AN

ACCOUNT

Of the late Dreadful

EARTHQUATE AND FIRE,

Which destroyed the

CITY OF *LISBON*,

The Metropolis of *Portugal*.

In a Letter from a Merchant Refident there,
to his Friend in England

———————————————
———————————————

London
Spradabach Publishing
2024

SPRADABACH PUBLISHING
BM Box Spradabach
London WC1N 3XX

An Account of the Dreadful Earthquake and Fire,
Which Destroyed the City of Lisbon, the Metropolis of Portugal.
In a Letter from a Merchant Resident there, to his Friend in England

First published in 1755

First Spradabach edition published 2024
© Spradabach Publishing 2024

Interior design by Alex Kurtagic

ISBN 978-1-909606-49-4

British Library Cataloguing-in-Publication Data:
A catalogue record for this book is available from the British Library.

Table of Contents

Note on This Edition

The present volume is based on the edition published in London by J. Payne in 1755. The text is reproduced in its entirety.

The spelling, punctuation, capitalisation, and italics have been left as in the original.

The illustrations have been added, obtained from contemporary sources, except for the depiction of Lisbon on page 3, which is from 1572.

An index has been generated.

An
Account
of the Dreadful
Earthquake and Fire,
Which Destroy'd
the City of Lisbon

Dear Sir,

I presume to imagine it will not a little gratify your Curiosity to receive, from an Eye-Witness thereof, some Account of the late dreadful EARTHQUAKE, which laid the Capital of *Portugal* in Ruins; and of the FIRE which thereupon broke out in several Parts of them at once, and (assisted by some wicked Incendiaries for the Sake of Plunder) burning furiously for five successive Days, reduced that whole Metropolis to Ashes; rendering it such a Spectacle of Terror and Amazement, as well as of Desolation to Beholders, as perhaps has not been equalled from the Foundation of the World! Of these, my Friend, I shall endeavour to give you a true Description; relying on the Veracity of my Narrative to atone for all Imperfections of Stile and Method: Particulars, that a Mind and Heart agitated as mine have been, must be supposed little capable of attending to, and therefore I only pretend to give you a simple Account of Things just as they happened, without any other Circumstance to recommend it to your serious Perusal, than the Importance of the Subject, and the Veracity of the Relation.

Lisbon in 1572.

It may, perhaps, be necessary previously to inform you, that the City of *Lisbon*, which was situated on the Northern Shore of the River *Tagus*, about six Leagues from the Sea, stood upon very uneven Ground, and also that its Streets and Buildings in general, were extremely irregular. A Valley between two high Hills, all covered thick with Edifices, is the general Description of the Place. The Valley which runs North and South, was undoubtedly the Seat of the ancient City: On the Side next the River of which stood the King's Palace, with a large open Square to the Eastward of it, sep-

Lisbon in 1740.

arated by some low Buildings, a small Fort and a Wall, from the principal Key of the City, and a much frequented sandy Beach: On the other Side of the Valley was another extensive Square called *Rocio*, in which there was held a daily Market, and a weekly Fair: And there was the Inquisition situated, the Church and Convent of St. *Dominick*, the Hospital, and other public as well as private other Buildings. The principal Streets of the City were between these two Squares, and the Middle of them might be reckoned the Centre of it. On the Summit of the Hill to the Eastern Side, was situated the Castle of St. *George*, or *Lisbon*, with a spacious Platform before it, surrounded by a parapet Wall which was planted thick with Cannon. And the whole Hill except Part of the Western Side of it was covered thick with Buildings, the Streets and Lanes of which, were most remarkably narrow. On the Hill to the Westward were many stately Buildings, particularly the Palace of *Braganza*, and in this Part of the Town the Streets were in general wider, the Buildings better, and the Prospects pleasanter than in either of the others. There were scattered about the various Parts of the City, many spacious Convents and princely Palaces of the Nobility: And of Churches and Chapels an innumerable Quantity, not extremely beautiful in their Architecture, but immensely rich in interior Ornaments. I shall not enlarge on the other publick or private Parts of that City which is now no more; having, I hope, given you an Idea of its Situation sufficient for my present Purpose. The Number of Souls it contained, I have heard rationally computed at about three hundred and fifty thousand.

It may be proper, likewise, here to inform you, that various have been the Opinions of People concerning the Time of Duration of the two violent Shocks of the Earthquake, and the Interval that was between them; which I, and many others, have estimated at a Quarter of an Hour, measuring it in our Imaginations by what we employed ourselves about from the Beginning to the Ending of that tremendous Visitation; during the Operations of which, as it pleased God to preserve my Mind in intire Composure, and its full firmness, I shall inform you of what past with me, and that perhaps will give you a tolerable Idea of the EARTHQUAKE and at the same time enable you to Judge of the Time of its duration.

I lived in a House not far from the Centre of the City, at a small eminence on the foot of the Hill, towards the Eastern side of it four Stories high, Our House was reckoning the ground Story for one, the two uppermost of which, as is usual in that City, served for the accommodation of our Family, the lower ones being alotted for the uses of Business, Stabling, &c. In the third Story was my Bed-chamber, and one of the two outermost next the Street of seven Rooms that were upon that Floor. There was I sitting on the first Day of the present Month, about ten of the Clock in the Morning, (the Weather being serene, and the Sky without a Cloud in it,) when I felt the House begin gently to shake; which gradually increased with a rushing noise, like the Sound of heavy Carriages, driving hard at some Distance, and such I at first imagined the Cause of the Noise and Shaking I heard and felt. But both of them gradually increasing, and observing the Pictures in my Room to flap against the Walls, I started up, and immediately perceived it was an EARTHQUAKE; and having never been sensible of the Shaking of one before, I stood a good while very composedly remarking its Operations; till from waving and shaking, I thought the Room began to roul, which made me run towards an inward one; more to the Centre of the House; but the Motion was then so extremely violent, that I with Difficulty, kept upon my Feet. Every part of the House cracked about me, the Tiles rattled on the Top of it; the Walls rent on every side; the Doors of a pretty large Book-case that stood in my Room, and which were locked, burst open, and the Books fell from the Shelves within it, but not till after I was got into the Room adjoining; and I heard, with Terror, the falling of Houses round about, and the Screams and Cries of People from every Quarter. At length, all beginning to settle into stilness again, I went into three or four Rooms of the Floor I was upon, to look for Servants, but finding none; concluded, with good reason, they had all left the House. So returning to my Room, I determined to change my Cloaths (for I was in a Night- Gown, Cap, and Slippers,) and go out also. I had drest my Legs, and was putting on my Coat and Waistcoat, (having first put up my Books in their Case and locked the Doors of it) when I felt the second Shock begin: So I snatched up my Hat, and taking my Wig from a Sconse, ran down one pair of Stairs and half way another, when I stopt short, on hearing Tiles and large Stones falling from the Top of our own House and another into a small yard I must past through. This made me reflect, that by flying from one falling House, I ran the risk of being buried under the Ruins of many others in the narrow Streets. I must be obliged to pass before I could get to any Place of greater Safety, so I determined to remain where I was, which was on a winding stone Staircase, each step of which was an entire Stone, of about the length of a Yard and an half; and this place I chose preferable to any over on the Consideration, that if the House fell, the Stones over my Head would put an immediate end to my Life, and prevent the more miserable Fate of being buried alive under Ruins. Here while I remained, the Steps I stood upon as well as those over my Head, lifted to a most shocking Degree, and I expected every Moment to be crushed to Death. Here, while I continued, I heard, from some part of the Yard below me, a mournful Voice groaning, and calling out for Help, with considerable intervening pauses, at least for a dozen Times before the shaking of the House, and the falling of Stones would permit my endeavour to offer any Assistance. Which when I found an opportunity for doing, I did, and discovered the Person in Distress was our own House-keeper, who in the first Shock, had endeavoured to run out of our House, with a Man Servant, but were met at the Street door by the Wall of a House falling from the opposite side of the Way, which wounded them both, but particularly the poor Woman, and half buried them in its Rubbish.

Now putting all these Particulars of Observation and Employment together, I leave you to judge if they could be well comprised within less time than a quarter of an Hour: And, indeed, from comparing my Calculation with those of some others, I find my Opinion confirmed concerning the time the two Shocks of the Earthquake and the Interval betwixt them lasted. There has also been another Dispute here about the exact time in which the first Tremor began. Some thinking it was before, others after ten of the Clock; but the greatest Number pronounce the Clock had not struck. And in Confirmation of their Opinion, I have seen a Letter from Cadiz, that mentioned the Shock's being felt there at fifty-seven Minutes after Nine: And as it was much less considerable there, it may, I think, be reasonably concluded to have happened something earlier at *Lisbon.*

The first Care that employed me after the great Shocks of the Earthquake were over, was to help our Housekeeper out of the Rubbish: When having fetched her down a Chair to fit in, I went myself and sent the wounded Servant (who was not greatly hurt) to look for Assistance to help her. But after many Trials, in vain, to get a Surgeon, I left her under the Care of an *Irish* Family in the Neighbourhood, and went over Heaps of Ruins to the large Square I have already described to be before the Palace, and by the Side of the River.

There I found Numbers of People, of all Nations, collected together; with such Signs of Terror and Distress in every Countenance as can be much better imagined than described. There were among them several Persons almost naked; one of which was an *English* Surgeon, with nothing on him but a Shirt, Cloak, and Pair of Slippers. I endeavoured to prevail on him to go and visit the poor Woman I had left behind me, by assuring him, that upon his asking for them, my Servant would supply him with a whole Suit of my Cloaths, and every thing else he was in need of (for he could get none of his own, the House he lived in being fallen down) and he promised me that he would go: But I believe the poor Man was terrified from doing it by what I am going to give an Account of; for he did not pay the Visit, as the poor

Woman has since told me, who fortunately escaped with her Life.

Not long after my Arrival at the Place I have mentioned, a general Pannic was raised from a Crowd of People's running from the Waterside, all crying out the Sea was pouring in and would certainly overwhelm the City. This new Alarm, created such Horrors in the agitated Minds of the Populace, that vast Numbers of them ran screaming into the ruinated City again, where, a fresh Shock of the Earthquake immediately following, many of them were buried in the Ruins of falling Buildings.

This Alarm was, however, not entirely without Foundation. For the Water of the River rose at once above twenty Feet perpendicular, and subsided again to its natural Pitch in less than a Minute's time. I was of the Number that continued where we were, but the Horror and Distraction of the Multitude were so increased by this astonishing Phænomena, that I confess they appeared more shocking to me than even the very Operations of the Earthquake. For instead of the Meltings of meeting Friends, the mutual Implorings of Pardon for all Offences, the Lamentations of Husbands for their Wives, Parents for their Offspring, Children for those who had given them Being, and all in general for their ruined Fortunes and Possessions, now there was nothing to be seen but Gatherings of Crowds

about Priests and Friars, all falling on their Knees, kissing the Earth, beating their Breasts, flapping their Cheeks, and crying out for Absolution, which was granted in general Terms to Hundreds of them at once.

The Rising of the Water, I guess, happened at about eleven of the Clock. And in this Scene of Anguish and Despair I continued till about twelve; when in a State of Restlessness and Anxiety, I removed to the Fish-Market, which was in the Neighbourhood. There I joined a disconsolate Family, who sat looking on the Ruins of their fallen House. I continued with them for some time: And, as it was a public Outlet from the City, observing many Persons whom we knew hurrying out of Town, I proposed to the Gentlemen to take the same Course, which they at first declined. But on my taking Leave of them they called me back, and, altering their Resolution, told me they would accompany me.

Of this mournful Society, there was no one but myself that had either Hat, Wig, Coat or Shoe, and we set forward without knowing whither we should go. At length we resolved to direct our Course to an *English* Gentleman's Country-house, about a League eastward of the City, who was so kind as to shelter us all for some Days till the greatest Part of our Company could get aboard Ships bound for *England*, but it is still the Habitation of myself and one of the Gentlemen that accompanied me, as well as of two other Families of Foreigners, and one of Natives.

In the Afternoon I returned with two other Gentlemen to the City, where I rejoiced in being the Means of saving some considerable Effects of a Friend, but could do nothing for myself. However, I went early the following Morning to my own House accompanied with two People, from whence with the utmost Difficulty and Hazard I saved some Books, Papers, and wearing Apparel, which was done with so much Fatigue, that one of my Companions got a dangerous Disorder from it, and I myself was not well for a Week after it. As soon as we had got those few things to a Place of Safety, another Attempt was however made for fetching more, but on the Arrival of the first Person who returned to the House, it was found to be on Fire; and as no Money could procure Assistance at any Time of that Calamity's Duration, I was forced to abandon my House and every Thing in it to the Fury of the merciless Flames.

I should have mentioned, that on our first leaving of the City, we perceived, by the Clouds of Smoke which we saw arise, that it had taken Fire; and we have since heard, from Persons who were upon Eminences when the Earthquake happened, that the two great . Shocks had been over very few Minutes, before they perceived the Ruins had taken Fire at six or seven different Places. The first that was observed, was at the Convent or Church of St. *Domingo's* in the *Rocio*: The second, at the *Boa-Hora*, near the Palace: The rest at other Parts of the City, which all raging with great Fury, and burning for five or six Days successively, reduced the whole Capital of *Portugal* to Ashes, except a few Houses at the Out-skirts of the Town, which are, however, so much shattered with the Earthquake, as to be unfit for other Service, than, by the Help of Props, to afford a present Shelter to Crowds that could otherwise have no Screen at all against the Inclemencies of Weather, which, in respect to Rain and piercing Winds, are frequently extremely severe in this Country during a great Part of the Winter Season.

The Loss of Lives from this dreadful and double Calamity, has doubtless been very great. There is no Possibility of ascertaining Numbers, because there was such a Hurry in clearing the City of such dead Bodies as could be got at, that no Accounts of them could be well taken. I have, in general, heard the Numbers killed by the Earthquake estimated at about thirty Thousand; and I have heard the Calculation carried by others much higher. The Disaster, it is certain, happened on one of the most unlucky Days in the whole Year, for the Circumstances of Slaughter and Fire, for it being the Days of *All Saints*, every Altar in every Church, Chapel, Convent and private House, was lighted up. The Time of the Day likewise, was another very unfortunate Particular, it being that in which most People went to their Devotions, which the Day made necessary to pay at every Altar. Thus were the Churches crouded with an extraordinary Concourse of People, who all continued an unusual Time within them; and happening at the Time of the Day most convenient for the Generality of People's attending divine Service, occasioned a terrible Slaughter, for there was scarce a Church or Chapel in the City whose Roof did not fall in with the Earthquake, and hardly one that at the same Time was not quite filled with People. To these Numbers, if we add those that perished within, Doors, and without from the falling of the Houses, and afterwards of those who from being wounded and whelmed under Ruins, were burnt to Death, and those who died afterwards of Wounds and Sickness got in this terrible Calamity, the Loss of Lives must be immense: But it is what, from the Nature of Things, a true Knowledge of can never be arrived at. As to the Fires, I have already mentioned that the two first that appeared were in Churches or Convents, and probably most others had their Beginnings at like Places, one account of the vast Numbers of Candles that were that Day burning within them. But I must, however, acquaint you that some Malefactors, since executed for plundering the Ruins, have confessed they fired, some Places in the City in order to facilitate their Scheme for Robbing: Yet there is no Reason to doubt that the first Fires began without the Help of Incendiaries, and that many of them, if not all had their Beginnings in the Churches.

Of the numerous Quantity of Protestants of many Nations who resided in that Metropolis, it is certain a very inconsiderable Number of them perished, and many of them I may with Truth and Decency, say, had almost miraculous Escapes. It was a Church-Day) to the *English* Factory, and the Clergyman who was to have performed Divine Service, was one who had been arrived but a very few Days from *England* for the Recovery of his Health. This Gentleman was, by Way of Physical-Exercise, walking upon the Platform of the Castle when the Earthquake began, and had, luckily for himself, strained Time to the utmost therein, on account of the extreme Fineness of the Morning. But as his Situation then saved him from the Danger of falling Buildings, or at least the Horror of feeing them tumble around him, it accidentally involved him in other Apprehensions, which, being singular in their Nature, I shall take upon me the Task of giving you a Relation of.

This poor Gentleman, being just arrived, could of course know nothing of the Language of the Country; and the *Portuguese* pronunciation of *Latin* being so very different from that used in *England*; the People of the two Nations cannot understand one another, even in the speaking of that Tongue. After the great Shocks of the Earthquake were over, and the People, who were on that Place and had fled to it, began to exercise themselves in acts of Penitence and Devotion, you may imagine a solitary Clergyman, whose Function and Religion he had reason to conclude were particularly obnoxious, and who had it hot in his Power, to make himself understood, or of understanding others, must conceive himself to be in a perilous Situation. And whether he shewed any signs of Apprehension that might fix their Attention upon him, or that any one informed them who, or what he was, or that it was a singular Zeal in the Crowd at that Place; or, in short, from what Notice there is no pretending to say, but the Multitude gathered about him, he apprehended to put an end to his Life; but he was for much mistaken, that it was from good Will to save his Soul, for the Priests that were with him fairly Baptized him without his knowing what they were about, till they came to the User of the Water in the Ceremony, and then it was in vain to resist. After they had accomplished their Work, the poor misguided Zealots expressed so wonderful a Regard and Fondness for their fancy'd Proselyte, that the Priests even proceeded to kneeling down before him and embracing his Knees, nay to the very kissing of his Feets. But however to do

Justice to the People of the Country, I must declare, this was the only act of violence that was offered to Foreigners of any Denomination, and this being mistakes only so, and attended with no Consequence whatever, ought rather to be considered as an Act of tender Affection; for it was in them poor ignorant Creatures (I conclude Priests and all) no other than a Desire to save, by an Act of kind. Compulsion, al Soul which they thought might other wife, be infallibly loft. And as a Proof that the Priests were, no wiser than their Lay-attendants in this fruit less Act of Piety, I must acquaint you that our Baptism is admitted to be vallid by the very Canons of the Church of *Rome*, as on this very occasion the *Pope*'s Nuncio has declared, as he has also done, that if he could discover who they were of the Clergy that assisted in the untimely and unnecessary Administration of that Sacrament, he would take upon him to see they were properly punished. If shall end my Account of this Adventure with acquainting you, that the word Minister in the Language of this Country as well as ours, is used in a double Sense when the Affair began to be noised abroad, the Abbess of a Nunnery wrote a congratulatory Letter to the *British* Envoy on his Conversion, and desired, as a Testimony of his true Catholicism, as suitable Charity for the Sisterhood under her Care; by which means, the Holy Mother encountred a Rebuke, and loft, by the claim of Piety, the Contribution which Humanity might otherwise have afforded.

But to return to my Account of this dreadful Calamity, I have now to mention that those who could observe the Motions of the Earth during the Shak-

ings of it, say, that its Wavings were East and West, which is the Course of the River *Tagus* from *Lisbon* to the Ocean. During the two violent Shocks of the Earthquake, the principal Key of the City, which was new, and built of a coarse Marble, in a manner extremely strong, for the Stones were not only crampt together with Irons, but also let into one another by Joints, so as to be made almost one solid Block, all sunk together (though the Tide ebbed before many Yards below the Foot of it) quite under Water, and so deep that no Pole could reach to the upper part of it. I have been since told (but with what Truth I cannot pretend to say) that having been tried with a Line, it is discovered to have sunk fifty Fathom below the Surface of the Water. So it is probable the whole Bed of the River is altered; for during the first Shocks, and an Hour before the Rising of the Water in so extraordinary a manner as I have described, several Boats passing on the River were seen to twirl round as in a Whirl-pool, and then, with their Sterns mounted out of the Water, plunged head foremost beneath it, without rising any more, at least within Eye-reach of the beholders. Several Stacks of Salt on the Banks of the River, many Leagues above *Lisbon*, sunk almost to their whole Height into the Ground, and so remain. The Earth opened in abundance of Places of the Kingdom. As at *Alcantara*, a League West of the City; at *Sacavem*, two Leagues to the North-East; at St. *Martinho*, fifteen Leagues towards the North West; at *Azeitam*, three Leagues to the South; and at *Setuval*, four Leagues towards the South-West of it. Not to mention Places at a greater Distance. Some of these Chasms remain yet open, others closed up again; out of some issued Water, from others came a sulphurous Vapour, and from others there proceeded nothing but Wind.

Concerning the Extent of this Earthquake and its Effects, we can say no more at present than that it was immensely great. All *Portugal* and most, if not all, the Kingdom of *Spain* felt it. Ships have arrived that felt it fifty Leagues at Sea, to the Westward. It was felt, we hear, at *Corke* in *Ireland*; and we are told there was a very considerable irregular Rising of the Sea at

Mounts-Bay in *Cornwall*. How it has fared with *France, Italy, Barbary,* and the *Western Islands,* we are impatient to learn, and are indeed under great Apprehensions for the Security of the latter.

It would be a vain Attempt to endeavour describing the numberless Miseries, and terrible Distresses of all kinds, occasioned by this dreadful Calamity, as well as the shocking Effects that it had on the Minds of all People. Infinite were the Numbers of poor broken-limbed Persons, who were forced to be deserted even by those who loved them best, and left to the miserable Torture of being burnt alive. Women big with Child were delivered in the open Fields and Places, amidst the Groans and Cries of trembling Multitudes. A large Number of Persons remained, some two, others three Days in the great Square by the

Palace, while that Edifice and every House round it was reduced to Ashes. Nay, the few Necessaries they had saved from their Houses, and which we scattered about the Place took Fire, and many helpless Persons were burnt to Death by them, while others were hurried from one Part to another with their Limbs broken, and for the Setting of which they had been able to get no Assistance, many in various Distempers, with which they were afflicted, and all distracted with Terrors, or sinking under the Anguish of Despair. In that Place, and in the midst of these Distresses, a poor Gentlewoman was delivered of Twins: Those about her, till they could find Means of escaping, did what they could to assist her, as I have been told by one who continued three Days there, but what at last became of her I know not. Numbers continue in the Fields till this time (as

do the whole Royal Family in the Gardens of one of the Palaces at Belem) partly for want of Houses to shelter them, and partly from Fear of trusting themselves under the Roofs of them, as there are sometimes Shakings of the Earth even to this Hour, which is in the twentieth Day from the Beginning of this disastrous Calamity.

In passing about the Boundaries of the City, for some Days after the Destruction of it, 'twas extremely affecting to receive the Congratulations on my Escape, from those who know me, and to observe those of others. For the first few Days the Natives seemed entirely taken up with Acts of Devotion and Repentance: Every Road and every Field were filled with People at Prayers, or in Processions. But Time, and a little rainy Weather, have turned some of their Thoughts to other necessary Duties; and now there begins to be an Appearance of Industry and Composure again.

I have past through the Ruins of the principal Parts of the City, and they are dreadful indeed to behold. I believe so compleat a Destruction has hardly befallen any Place on Earth, since the Overthrow of Sodom and *Gomorrah.*

The *British* Factory here, upon this melancholy Occasion, have acted with Wisdom and Honour worthy of their Country. They, like those of all oth-

The Opera House.

er Nations, are almost all ruined: Yet such as had any Warehouses of Provisions by them, went immediately and offered them on the most reasonable Terms to the King, who accepted the Offer with great Marks of Approbation. Such a Resolution not only discovered a humane Disposition in themselves, but was a Proof of great Prudence also; for amidst an unhoused and distracted People, there was no Security for Property of that kind, especially if the Owners of them had pretended to stand upon Terms. And as soon as the Factory could be assembled, they unanimously resolved upon presenting to his Most Faithful Majesty the following Address.

SIRE,

The Consul-General and Merchants, Subjects of his Britannic Majesty, beg Leave to offer, at your royal Feet, their sincere Condolance on the late Calamity which the Almighty hath permitted to befal your capital City, and several other Parts of your Majesty's Dominions.

Truly sensible, as they are, of your Majesty's gracious Disposition, and grateful for the repeated Instances they have received of your Royal Protection, they beg Leave to assure your Majesty of their chearful and determined Resolution to prosecute, under your auspicious Influence and sovereign Justice, a Commerce so particularly necessary at this Time, and always so advantageous to the Kingdoms of *Great-Britain* and *Portugal*.

They think it, in a peculiar manner, their Duty to express the strong Reliance they have on your Majesty's princely Care for making such wife Regulations for the Security of Commerce, and Re-establishment of Mercantile Credit, as may fix them on the justest and firmest Foundations: Such as may, by their public Utility, reflect the brightest Glory on your Royal Name, and make your Dominions prosperous and happy to the latest Posterity.

This Address was presented to his *Portugese* Majesty on the following Day, in the Language of his Country, by the *British* Consul, introduced by his Majesty's Envoy at that Court. It was most graciously received by the King, and highly approved of by his Minister. And that the Merit of it may rest, where it ought to do, let me acquaint you that it was singly thought of, and drawn up by that Man who was lately so illegally and barbarously persecuted by the Court of *Portugal*, and happened to be presented on the very Day which, two Years before, he had been banished that Kingdom, without a Crime, and unheard in his Defence; a Sacrifice as its supposed to private Malice, to the Dishonour of his *Portuguese* Majesty, the Disgrace of Justice, and the Prejudice of unshaken Integrity and unsullied Innocence.

I may perhaps trouble you with a second Letter on the Consequences of this fatal Affair, not only to *Portugal*, but also to *Great-Britain* and other trading Nations in *Europe*, which I hope a more composed Mind may make less imperfect than that I now trouble you with, who am,

Dear Sir,

Your most faithful

and obedient Servant.

MARVILLA,
Nov. 20, 1755.

FINIS

Index

www.ingramcontent.com/pod-product-compliance
Lightning Source LLC
Chambersburg PA
CBHW020347100426
42812CB00035B/3387/J